Crossing the Finish Line:

GETTING TO THE TOP AND STAYING THERE

Accelerating Your Career in the "New Normal" World

Crossing the Finish Line:

GETTING TO THE TOP AND STAYING THERE

Accelerating Your Career in the "New Normal" World

ADDIE PERKINS WILLIAMSON, PH.D.

ISBN: 978-1-4834-0159-1 (sc)
ISBN: 978-1-4834-0158-4 (e)

Lulu Publishing Services rev. date: 06/18/2013

This book is dedicated to all the women and men around the world with a strong desire to maximize their career success

Dedicated with much love to my daughter,
Nicole Alexandra Williamson

Table of Contents

Part 3. Everyone Gets into Trouble at Some Point

Acknowledgments

This book had what can only be described as a long gestation period. During that time, my dreams of actually completing this book were sustained by a number of supportive family, dear friends, and colleagues. Among them, I would be remiss if I did not mention my daughter, Nicole Williamson, and my siblings Joseph Perkins, Doretha Perkins, and James Perkins. Arisa Cunningham, Linda DiMarino, Deborah Elam (who first suggested I write this book,) Erika Hayes James, Susan Johnson, Suzanne Randolph, and David Thomas—while beleaguered by me during those long years—remained strong, staunch supporters. Marge Kearns gave me the final push, for which I shall always be grateful, and Toni Sciarra Poynter, my editor, made it all come together and make sense. The team at Lulu Publishing was simply outstanding and I want to thank Cara Lockridge for making the process as painless as possible.

For those of you I did not mention, know that my heart remembers even if my brain missed a step. I am sincerely grateful to all of you for helping me finally get here.

Introduction:
The Landscape in the "New Normal" Workplace

Welcome to the "New Normal."

It's the world we live in now, thanks to the global economic crisis and turmoil that we've experienced the last few years and that continue to plague us. It's called the "New Normal" as a warning to those who thought that in just a couple of years, we'd somehow return to the "good old days" of business and life before the economic meltdown.

We're still waiting.

The "New Normal" is our new reality, our new way of life, and we had all better get used to it. Virtually every company, law firm, government agency, university, school, medical facility, for-profit, and not-for-profit organization has been affected. No one was left untouched, and no one is the same.

Many organizations did not survive this journey. The companies—and people—who did survive were flexible, adaptable, proactive, and on top of their game. Companies survived by reducing headcount, reorganizing and restructuring, figuring out what was really important, learning to "see around corners," and initiating a host of other measures to keep their doors open. People who survived quickly learned the new rules and played the game better than everyone else.

As I write this, our competitive marketplace has changed dramatically as our traditional sources of revenue and growth have shifted offshore and to parts of the world where we previously have had little presence. That shift has helped shape the "post-Great-Recession environment" that we currently experience. It has affected in some way virtually every person living and working in this country—including you. It has resulted in significant changes in assumptions, strategies, and approaches for winning in the global marketplace, with comparable changes in expectations for who gets ahead in this "new normal" workplace.

So, where does that leave those of us interested in not just surviving, but thriving, in this environment? What does it take to get to the top and stay there—however we define it? I'm glad you asked.

You no doubt committed yourself to success long ago, maybe at the very beginning of your career. Otherwise, how would you have gotten to the point where you are now, poised to advance to the highest levels?

By reading this book, you have recommitted yourself to reaching those higher goals. You know that you can't afford many missteps, particularly if you are a multicultural man or woman. A misstep now may mean a future stuck at midlevel or the possibility of career derailment (yes, it happens, and I discuss it in Chapter 11).

You have watched and you have learned, but it's possible no one has ever sat you down and said, "Here are the rules and the way things work at the very top of the corporate ladder."

The executive women and men in my seminars really snap to attention when we come to "the unwritten rules in corporate America." They know that if they're ignorant of these unwritten rules, they're almost guaranteed to trip over them. And tripping over them is a sign that you don't really understand "the game" or play it well. It may also make executives in positions of power think twice before mentoring or sponsoring you.

There are any number of ways someone can trip over the unwritten rules or experience career derailment. There's the guy who contradicts his boss in front of others rather than tactfully making his point in private; the woman who puts on her makeup in her car in the parking lot as colleagues walk by instead of arriving well-groomed and pulled together; the guy who delivers his project late amid excuses compared to the one who delivers on time (or early) and on budget; the woman who looks tongue-tied when the CEO says "Good morning" in the elevator instead of being ready with a poised response.

Minor failings are never overlooked; each instance contributes to an overall image of ineffectiveness. But minor successes are like compound interest: they build upon each other and eventually create the impression that you're ready for major responsibility and power.

In Part I we review the importance of outstanding performance as a critical building block for your career success, and how best to achieve it. We then tackle "The Big Six" success factors that accelerate your career once outstanding performance is a given. In Part II we examine eight of the more important rules you must play by in order to succeed in almost any company culture. In Part III we help you understand what might cause your career to stall or derail and how to quickly get it back on track. Along the way are "self-coaching" exercises to help you apply what you've learned to your own career. From this page forward, I commit myself to your career success. I hope you will make the same commitment to accelerating your career.

PART I

Building Blocks for Career Success

Chapter 1:
Outstanding Performance:
Your Ticket to the Game

Remember, no one is irreplaceable. Outstanding performance is your entry ticket into the high-stakes game of getting to the top and staying there. Typically, people on this fast-track but often perilous road to the top have to perform 20% better than everyone else—and that is particularly true for women and people of color. Your performance is key in building your brand or image, gaining exposure and visibility, and thus attracting necessary mentors and sponsors. Performance is your ticket to the game.

With few exceptions, no one gets ahead with lackluster or mediocre performance. People who consistently deliver results, whatever the challenges or circumstances, typically get ahead. Your successful performance will garner the relationships and visibility you need for promotion to the highest levels. And there are techniques you can use to ensure that your performance is perceived as outstanding. It starts with your Performance Plan.

Your Performance Plan

Your goal every year is to have your boss give you the highest rating possible on your performance appraisal. That will not happen unless you carefully manage the entire process, from the selection of goals and objectives to the writing of your performance appraisal. Yes, this is *your* process to manage if you want the outcomes you desire. Here's how it works.

Every company has a set of expectations of each person it employs. Those expectations may be conveyed formally or informally. Larger organizations typically have a formal performance-management process with goals and objectives, development plans, and a structured review procedure. In smaller companies, a more informal process may be used, with expectations conveyed in a casual conversation.

Whether the process at your workplace is formal or informal, your first and primary task is to ensure that you and your boss are on the same page about what is expected of you in your current position for the current year. Do your homework. For example:

1. Find out what the overall goals and priorities are for the company and your business unit or function.

2. What are your boss's goals, objectives, and priorities?

3. How do your department and your work fit into those goals and priorities?

4. What can you contribute from where you sit? Another way of asking this is: what can you deliver that directly aligns with the most critical priorities of the business, your function, and your boss?

I always counsel my clients to ensure that at least 75% of their goals and objectives are in direct support of their boss's goals and objectives. Review your goals. Are they 75% aligned with your boss's goals and top priorities? If not, go back to the drawing board. My 75% rule is designed to ensure that your goals and objectives demonstrate your commitment to your boss's success, and that you are working on what your boss considers the most important problems and opportunities for the business. It also helps ensure that your work is "close to the center of gravity" of the business—that is, central and critical to the business's #1 and

#2 priorities. When your work is close to the center of gravity, you're more likely to be invited to the important meetings and are in position to become one of your boss's primary go-to people and potentially a member of your boss's inner circle, or "kitchen cabinet". Therefore, prepare yourself for writing your goals and objectives by having a conversation with your boss about what you are expected to accomplish and contribute and how that aligns with what he or she is expected to accomplish.

As you develop a set of goals and objectives for yourself and for your department (if you manage others), make sure your goals are challenging, involve a bit of risk, and require you to try new things. There is no way to consistently achieve an outstanding performance rating by doing the same old things year after year. Look for ways to take your game and your results to the next level. Every year the bar is raised (or should be), and you must move out of your comfort zone at some level to accommodate it. Always include at least one goal that continues your professional development.

You may have heard that goals should be SMART: Specific, Manageable, Actionable, Realistic, and Time-Bound. Developing SMART goals helps ensure that your goals are 1) described in sufficient detail to be understandable and make sense, and 2) are manageable in scope; that is, doable in the time allowed and with the resources available. Having SMART goals can make you less likely to over-promise and under-deliver (a huge stressor for you, and the kiss of death to your career.)

Your Performance Plan Meeting

During the meeting with your boss to review your goals and objectives, you want to accomplish two things:

1. agree on the appropriateness of your goals and objectives, and

2. determine what your boss will consider outstanding results.

In preparation for this meeting, you will have developed your suggested list of goals and objectives for the year based on your understanding of the goals and priorities for the business and your boss. Clarify the quality (how well) and the quantity (how much) requirements. Confirm the timeline and milestones for the delivery of each objective. Gather any other pertinent information you need to ensure that you clearly understand exactly what your boss is looking for in terms of activity, process, and results.

Based on your discussions during your meeting with your boss, finalize your Performance Plan. Use your company's procedure and materials if they exist; otherwise, create a straightforward document that describes in appropriate detail each goal or objective that you and your boss agreed on; the deliverable(s), the timeline, and the milestones; how the accomplishment of each goal will be measured, and what constitutes outstanding performance as opposed to good performance. Send that document to your boss as a recap of the meeting for his or her files. If you manage a staff, share your goals and objectives with them as appropriate and work with them to ensure their goals are 75% in direct support of your goals.

Now, Execute

A Performance Plan is necessary and helpful, but execution is essential. You must turn your goals and objectives into results. You must, essentially, deliver on the promise. Nothing beats results. Truly savvy bosses will not be fooled by activity that doesn't lead to desirable outcomes. They really will not care that you work 14-hour days if you don't deliver the results promised and expected. In fact, no one gets to the top without demonstrating an ability to consistently deliver not just results, but better-than-expected results year after year.

If you find yourself having difficulty delivering the results you expected, examine every aspect of your process. Where are things breaking down? Is it an underperforming person? A workflow bottleneck? Lack of relationship with the people you need to do the work or help you do it? Figure out what it is and fix it—immediately. You cannot afford a single year of less-than-superior results.

Tracking Progress: The Monthly Status Update

As we all know, things can change in the course of just 30 days. Emergency projects appear from nowhere… team members leave or are let go… senior management reshuffles the priorities… budget cuts necessitate changes in programs or projects. For your own records, I think it is extremely helpful to create a Monthly Status Update document that captures the activities, milestones, and results you (and your team) accomplished during the past 30 days. A synopsis can be sent to your boss for his or her reference and files, and a summary can be sent to your staff as well. These monthly updates will be immeasurably helpful at mid-year and year-end as you write your mid-year and end-of-year performance self-appraisals and the performance appraisals of your staff.

Tracking Progress: The Mid-Year Review

I believe strongly in a mid-year review, whether or not your company mandates it. Arrange a meeting with your boss to review your goals and objectives mid-way through your fiscal year. The mid-year review is designed to ensure that your goals and objectives are still directly tied to the priorities of the business and your boss. If there have been shifts in emphasis and priority, revise your goals and objectives to reflect those shifts. If there have been changes in the expectations of the quality or quantity of your deliverables, make sure your goals and objectives reflect those shifts.

Use the meeting to gain a sense of how well your boss thinks you're executing your Performance Plan. What's working well? Not so well? What changes need to be made? Does your boss still have the same description of what constitutes outstanding performance?

Don't be afraid to ask your boss if your performance is on track and how he or she would rate it at this point. And don't be alarmed if your boss is not as positive as you would like. The point of having a mid-year review is that it gives you 4 to 5 months to course- correct, if necessary, to upgrade your performance, and deliver outstanding results.

After the meeting, revise your Performance Plan and send it to your boss as a recap and for his or her files.

Your End-of-Year Performance Appraisal

If you set up these interim conversations and records, your performance rating/evaluation shouldn't hold any unpleasant surprises. Rather, it should be more a culmination of a series of professional and productive conversations you've had with your boss all year long. Throughout the year, your monthly updates and your mid-year review should have provided ample opportunities for discussion with and feedback from your boss on his or her perceptions of your performance.

Think of the performance appraisal as your opportunity to clarify the value you've added to the business throughout the year.

The key here is to focus on results, not activity! Now's the time to describe what you've delivered and its impact on the business. Quantify, quantify. What results have you accomplished on your own, working on a team, and/or working with your staff? Be clear and specific, and link all results back to the goals and objectives you and your boss agreed on at the beginning of the year or that you revised together along the way. If major obstacles were overcome, or if there were obstacles impossible to overcome, describe those and their impact on your results (but avoid at all costs making excuses). Pull out the monthly updates you created and your mid-year self-appraisal as supporting documents. Review the criteria your boss uses to judge outstanding performance. How close did you get to those targets—or better yet, how much did you exceed them?

Many companies allow you to have input into the performance appraisal your boss writes by having you first write and submit a self-appraisal. Always write a self-appraisal and submit it to your boss, even if your company has no formal process for doing so. It's your best opportunity for presenting your case for an outstanding performance appraisal.

Write your self-appraisal using the same format and language your boss would use to write your actual performance appraisal. Describe your goals, objectives, accomplishments, and results (remember: not activities!) as specifically and in as much detail as necessary so it's perfectly clear to anyone who will read it—i.e., your boss, the boss' boss, HR, and any others. Provide a suggested (but realistic) rating—and let's hope your work merits an "outstanding". You want to write your self-appraisal so well that your boss makes a few minor editorial revisions and then submits it pretty much as you wrote it.

And that's how you take control of your performance review!

The key to ensuring outstanding performance appraisals year after year is to manage the process carefully from beginning to end. You can do that by working with your boss to develop realistic but challenging goals and objectives that are in direct support of your boss's critical goals, the accomplishment of which will merit an outstanding performance rating. Then, together, you update those goals and objectives regularly as assignments and priorities change. So, to summarize:

- Keep track of your accomplishments with monthly status update reports.

- Do a mid-year check by creating and reviewing with your boss a mid-year self-appraisal.

- Write an end-of-year self-appraisal that your boss can easily submit as your formal performance appraisal.

- Perform, perform, perform so your work merits an outstanding performance rating.

While outstanding performance is a critical pre-requisite for success, performance alone is not enough to get to the top and stay there. In most companies, once you reach middle and upper middle management, variables other than performance come into play. At that point in an executive's career, strong, consistent performance is a given, and the need for "soft" skills becomes more prominent. One of those skills is the ability to recognize, acknowledge, and play the game exceedingly well.

Chapter 1
Self-Coaching and
Development Assignment:

Understanding How the Performance Management
System Really Works in Your Company
The Self-Coaching Concept

While you'll learn a great deal in this book about how to effectively identify and work with a coach, I also want you to understand the importance of the concept of "self-coaching"—that is, teaching yourself to identify your knowledge and skill gaps, and then finding ways to close those gaps.

You've coached yourself on any number of occasions: when you taught yourself to use the new phone, social media account, or data storage system your company now uses. As your own career coach, you'll use the concepts in a particular chapter to change or improve the way you operate in your workplace.

Each assignment will ask you to take some particular action and then assess the impact of that change on your success. In this first assignment, you'll focus on ensuring that your performance is perceived as outstanding by people critical to your career success—your boss, your boss's boss, and his or her boss. Many people underestimate their ability to achieve a performance appraisal that will get them noticed and enhance their eligibility for the promotion they want. I want you to never underestimate yourself.

First, Understand the Process

1. Who is responsible for the performance management process in your company?

2. What is included in the performance management process? For example:

    - goal setting?

    - development planning?

    - performance assessment?

    - succession planning?

    - compensation?

    - rewards and recognition?

3. What is the cycle or the timing for each part of the process?

4. Who has input into your performance appraisal?

    - You, via a self-appraisal?

    - Your customers?

    - Your peers?

    - Your boss?

    - Your boss's boss?

5. How strong is your relationship with each of the persons who will contribute to your performance rating?

6. How and when does each person provide input?

7. How and when is the best time for you to provide input to them?

8. What happens to your performance appraisal once your boss completes it?

- Who sees it next?

- How and when do you review and receive feedback from your boss?

- How do you plan for improvement?

9. Is your performance appraisal reviewed during succession planning in your company?

- Who participates in the succession planning meeting where you and your next job are discussed?

- What are the characteristics (i.e., ratings, results, readiness, relationships) of the people who are viewed most positively during those succession planning discussions?

- How is feedback provided regarding the outcome of the discussion about you during the succession planning meeting?

Now Master the Process and Make It Work for You

There is no need to wait. Begin immediately, wherever you are in your company's cycle, to use the performance management system to your advantage. Here are some suggestions to guide you:

1. Understand what is expected of your boss by his or her boss.

- Get a copy of your boss's goals and objectives and, if possible, a copy of the goals and objectives your boss's boss. You should also have available your company's and department's priorities and goals for the year.

- Write a one-paragraph description of your boss's critical

goals and objectives and how they support the business and his or her boss's objectives.

- Now write a second paragraph that describes how your goals and objectives fully support your boss's goals and objectives. If you find that your current goals and objectives are not in full support of your boss's critical goals and objectives, go no further with this exercise until you revise your goals and objectives accordingly.

2. Next, gain agreement with your boss on your goals and objectives for the year and their alignment with his or her goals.

- Take the time to have a good discussion or series of discussions with your boss about the critical tasks and projects you should work on this year. Do not shortchange this discussion. There is no more important discussion for the advancement of your career.

- Have on hand a list of your current tasks and projects. Clarify how those tasks and projects help your boss achieve his or her goals and the business achieve its goals. If you see no clear or direct link between what you are asked to accomplish and what is important for the business and your boss to accomplish, strike that task from the list and find a project that is directly linked to a critical project for your boss and the business.

- After you have a final list of goals, objectives, projects, and activities for the year; ask your boss what specifically you will have to deliver in order to receive an outstanding performance rating. This is a time for specificity versus vagueness. Resist the idea that your boss "will know it when he or she sees it." Most times they won't. Keep talking until the two of you agree on how outstanding performance looks. The better your relationship with your boss, the easier you'll find this conversation... but more on that later.

3. What feedback did you receive from your boss or your customer in your recent meetings?

   • What is the size of the gap between how you would like your performance to be perceived and how it is actually perceived according to the feedback you received?

   • What is the best way to close the gap?

   • What is the size of the gap between your company's assessment of your career potential and readiness for the next job/level and your own assessment?

   • What is the best way to close the gap?

Establish a Regular Feedback Loop

Feedback is critical for knowing what you're doing that's working well... and not so well. As busy as you both are, try to build in at least 15 to 20 minutes every month with your boss discussing nothing but how your performance is tracking.

This is where your Monthly Status Update is particularly helpful. Keep this document to one page so it's an easy read, upbeat and positive. At first, the steps outlined below may seem time-consuming and onerous. I promise after the first few months, it will get easier and you will appreciate how critical this process is to your career.

1. At the end of every month, create a Monthly Status Update document that captures the activities, milestones, and results accomplished during the past 30 days.

- If you are an individual contributor, you'll focus on your goals, activities, milestones, accomplishments, and results.

- For goals that required you to partner with other individuals, groups, or departments; list the deliverable(s), who was involved, what was accomplished, and your particular contribution.

- If you manage others, your Monthly Status Update should include the goals, activities, milestones, accomplishments, and results of the entire department for the month.

- For goals that require your department to partner with other individuals, groups, or departments; list the deliverable(s), who was involved, what was accomplished, and your department's particular contribution.

2. Send a synopsis of your Monthly Status Update to your boss for his or her reference and files and soliciting any comments, questions, or concerns.

- Try to turn any comments, questions, or concerns into an opportunity to receive and give feedback to your boss about what would help improve your performance.

- Always keep the conversation upbeat and pleasant so your boss has a positive perception of the experience. Demonstrate appreciation for his or her feedback as a gift, and change your behavior as appropriate.

- Now you have additional insight into how your performance is perceived and can make any changes necessary to ensure an outstanding performance rating.

3. Send a summary of your Monthly Status Update to your staff as well.

   - These monthly updates will help your staff better understand how to keep their goals aligned with yours.

   - It will also help them correct any misunderstanding you may have about their goals, activities, and accomplishments.

   - It will help you keep track of all of the assignments on their plates, particularly if you have a culture where people give assignments directly to your staff without notifying you first.

   - You will breathe a huge sigh of relief at mid-year and year-end when these reports provide you with rich, detailed information for giving feedback and writing performance appraisals.

4. Your Monthly Status Update is a great way to enhance your visibility and exposure and build relationships within the company.

   - Write your Monthly Status Update so that the accomplishments of your partners are suitably acknowledged.

   - Send a synopsis to the individuals involved and to their managers. While the individuals and managers will appreciate your giving them credit, doing this also provides visibility and exposure for you and your staff. (More on why visibility and exposure are so important later).

Chapter 2:
The Big Six – What It Takes to Get to the Top

For the 30 years I have been researching and studying the workplace, the following six success factors have been critical:

1. **Hard Work**: I cannot think of anyone who has risen to the top of his or her field without many years of consistent hard work. I've never been able to discern any shortcuts. That means putting in the time and energy necessary to get the job done exceptionally well. The closer you get to the top, the more likely you'll need to put in long hours: early mornings, full days, late evenings, weekends, and even working during holidays and vacations. As the stakes grow higher, so do the demands and expectations. The words hard work and sacrifice are often used together because they often go hand in hand. Getting to the top is not for the faint-of-heart. You need to be intentional and determined in order to succeed. Hard work is the first pre-requisite.

   As you make decisions about where to focus your efforts (also known as prioritizing), begin with the projects that are most important to your boss, your boss's boss, and the overall business. Chapter 1 provides a way to help you accomplish this. Avoid working on projects no one (particularly your boss) seems to be interested in. If your project is never discussed during staff meetings or during your one-on-one meetings with your boss, you may be working on something off the beaten path and therefore not important enough to warrant your hard work. Refocus your energies on the two or three things that always turn up on the staff meeting agenda or on issues your boss often brings up. Find a way to add value to those projects from where you sit.

As we discussed in Chapter 1, take the time to clarify with your boss what is expected and what represents outstanding work. As deadlines, deliverables, and quantity and/or quality expectations change, re-contract with your boss to ensure that you're working on the most salient projects and that the work you deliver is considered exemplary.

2. **Results**: It is very important not to confuse activity with accomplishment or outcomes. Employers are looking for outcomes—specifically, the results you committed to at the beginning of your fiscal year, as outlined in your annual goals and objectives. And they must be outstanding results, consistently delivered. For example, making phone calls to solicit business is an activity. Generating $1 million in new business as a result of those phone solicitations is an outcome. You will be successful to the extent that you deliver not only activity, but results or outcomes. Finally, remember that WHAT you do (your activities and results) and HOW you do it (your behaviors and leadership) are equally important for success at the most senior levels. Those who consistently exceed expected results using acceptable behaviors and leadership are typically most successful in any organization.

3. **Mentor and Sponsor**: Having both a mentor and a sponsor are essential for career success, and I make a distinction

between them, as they play different roles. A mentor is someone who consciously and purposely devotes the time and attention required to make you more effective and successful in your career. Mentors are typically more experienced, seasoned, often senior executives, although peers, colleagues, bosses, and even direct reports or seasoned admins can serve as mentors.

A mentor should be able to provide knowledge, skills, and/or support in areas where you require further development for continued success and upward mobility. One critical role of the mentor is to teach you how to successfully navigate at more senior levels in the organization—how to understand the rules and the players so you don't make an avoidable mistake.

Most successful people have several mentors simultaneously. The best mentor for you depends on your development needs. As you review your opportunities for further development, you'll likely find that no one mentor can assist you with everything you need to know. Perhaps one mentor might help you with how to present effectively to senior executives, while another might offer insights on leading and managing a global team. A mentor may often serve as a sounding board, coach, confidante, provider of feedback, or skilled interpreter of early warning signals.

Another reason to have more than one mentor is that, given the unpredictability of many organizations today, you may lose your mentor to downsizing, restructuring, reorganization, a move to another company, or retirement. Hedge your bets by having several mentors, both inside and outside the company.

Finally, a successful mentoring relationship is a give-and-take relationship. Both parties give and receive something they value. You may think you have nothing to offer a more senior leader, but that's not the case. Senior leaders are often disconnected from the day-to-day operations of the organization and thus out of touch with key opportunities and concerns. You may be in a position to provide this critical information, keeping the senior leader abreast of current perceptions and trends. In Chapter 9, I provide more detailed information on how to build and maintain an effective mentoring relationship.

A sponsor, on the other hand, is someone who can give you a job, a promotion, or can influence someone else to give it to you. A sponsor may have spent little or no time with you and may not personally know you, but will have experienced or heard about the quality of your work and results from a trusted source and is impressed with your performance.

Unless your next job is a lateral position, your boss cannot serve as your sponsor. For a promotion to a position at your boss's level, you need to be pulled up by someone who is at least two levels above you. So, in general, a sponsor should be someone at least two levels senior to you. Are you confident that your work is being seen by people two levels above you—by, say, executives at the level of your boss's boss? Here again, we come back to the importance of working hard on the right projects: the more critical your work is to the business, the higher its quality, and the more impressive your results, the more likely it is that senior executives will be exposed to your work. Simply put: mentors and sponsors are attracted to winners. Are you a winner?

4. **Networking and Relationships**: I believe wholeheartedly that relationships make the world go 'round. While each of us has a role to play at work, relationship trumps official role every time. If you need a favor or information from someone in your organization, you know that the likelihood of being granted that favor or getting that information directly corresponds to the strength of your relationship with that person.

Frank, Gail, and Bill work together at XYZ company. Frank and Gail took a business trip together, and now both have hefty travel expenses on their credit card bills, which are due in less than 30 days. They'd like to be reimbursed a bit early so they have the cash on hand to pay their credit card bills on time. XYZ's

Bill runs the department that manages travel reimbursement and is a stickler for maintaining company policy—"else chaos will reign," as he likes to say. Frank and Gail each call Bill to request expedited reimbursement. Frank receives an e-mail from Bill restating company policy. Gail receives a call from Bill admonishing her for operating outside company policy and promising that he'll expedite payment "this time, but never again!"

What's the difference? Bill doesn't know Frank. But Frank and Gail worked together on a project several years ago, developed a great relationship, and have maintained it ever since.

Most senior executives (and people in general) surround themselves with people they trust and with whom they have strong, long-standing relationships. Think about your relationships with family, colleagues, and friends. Don't relationships make your world go 'round as well?

The sum total of your relationships constitutes your network. The words "network" and "networking" are overused, but both are essential to success. A strong network provides information, access, resources, support, and intelligence. Last but certainly not least, great relationships make your work more enjoyable.

Many people tell me they dread the thought of "networking." Yet we do it all the time in both our personal and professional lives. We network when we call Aunt Sally to wish her a happy birthday. We network when we strike up a conversation with someone in the checkout line and end up exchanging contact information. We network when we send out holiday cards. We network when on Monday morning we take the time to ask how colleagues spent their weekends. We network when a colleague is promoted and we send an e-mail of congratulations. We network when we arrive early for a meeting and spend time chatting with other colleagues. We network when we go to a work-related cocktail party (or after-work drinks) and meet at least one person we didn't know or reconnect with someone we haven't seen or spoken with in a while. We network when we spend down-time friends, family, or colleagues during the weekend. Consciously or unconsciously, we network all the time. To get to the top and stay there, the idea is to network strategically; that is, with a purpose.

Networking professionally is crucial because, all things being equal, most people prefer to do business with people they know and feel comfortable with. Essentially, networking is all about making a connection—finding something in common with the other person. Making a connection with you will be much easier if you're friendly, engaging, and willing to give value first (e.g., information, opportunity, introduction, assistance) before you ask for something. The more connected people feel with you, the stronger and more helpful your network will be.

The best strategic networkers I know do these ten things:

1. Cultivate relationships and offer value

2. Network even when they don't need anything in return

3. Dedicate a specific amount of time each day or week to networking and find ways to enjoy it

4. Pick the right events and identify the people they want to meet

5. Establish rapport and find common ground with the people they meet

6. Show interest in what others do and get others interested in what they do

7. Make themselves memorable and remember something about the people they meet

8. Exchange contact information (and write a memory jogger on the other person's business card or v-card)

9. Move on to the next person after about 3 to 5 minutes so as not to monopolize that person's time (or be monopolized themselves)

10. Do what they say they are going to do and follow up within 24 to 48 hours

11. **Visibility and Exposure:** If you do outstanding work that no one sees and no one knows about, how much will it help your career? You and your work must be visible to the right people in order to advance your career (and if you want a mentor or a sponsor). People need to see what you can do in order to consider you for special projects, task forces, developmental opportunities, training, promotions, and other experiences that will help you advance.

When you have these exposure opportunities, you need to make sure that you effectively and strategically network. Suppose you're participating in a meeting with senior executives from several different departments. Whom would you target to meet and develop a connection? If you're employed in a large, decentralized company, using exposure opportunities to network is essential; otherwise, there's no way to make connections with people in other departments, divisions, and offices. If you're interested in making a lateral move or in relocating, there may be limited opportunities to meet people in that department or part of the world. Networking helps you use connections to make other connections.

Please note I am not suggesting that you should only interact with other people to meet your own professional needs. We include people in our network for a variety of reasons, not all associated with work. However, non-work relationships can often help us professionally. In fact, we almost never really know where our next golden opportunity will come from—but it's almost 100% certain it will come from or through someone who knows and likes us. That's why networking encourages us to build and maintain both personal and professional relationships with a wide variety of people with whom we have something in common and whose company we enjoy.

12. **Loyalty and Commitment**: At all levels, loyalty and commitment to the firm are expected. At the most senior levels, loyalty to the senior leader is essential and contributes to the strength of the relationship. As mentioned, most people like to surround themselves and interact with people they trust and feel comfortable with. Your loyalty and commitment will facilitate building the trusting relationships that can catapult you into the boss's "kitchen cabinet." The reward for membership in that inner circle is access to inside information and first choice of the best assignments and promotions.

SUCCESS FACTORS FOR THE NEW NORMAL WORLD

In addition to the Big Six, there are a few other success factors that have come into play in the post-Great Recession workplace. They may sound familiar—especially if you've survived downturns in the past. The key difference in our current environment is the global scope of the challenges, and the imperative of finding solutions that have a clear bottom-line impact.

- **Stay ahead of the now-truly global competition**: Some companies have always had a global focus, but most companies now find they're competing with new players in China, Brazil, and India where previously the field was primarily Europe-based. The interdependence of our economies means that no one has the luxury of taking a U.S.-centric approach. We are now all global citizens competing in a multitude of markets. As one CEO described it, we now have to "see around corners." Your ability to demonstrate in-depth knowledge of areas of the world critical to the success of your business will serve you well.

- **Demonstrate business savvy in a variety of market conditions**: In recent history we have had to successfully navigate through good and dismal economies, turnaround and cash cow situations, and markets large, small, and even some unheard-of. Success in the new normal means being agile, nimble, and a constant learner. This is the time for being proactive, taking calculated risks, offering new ideas, standing your ground regarding your ideas, having passion and conviction, and believing in yourself and your team.

- **Drive performance, despite challenges**: In many instances this means delivering excellence with significantly reduced staff and resources. Nevertheless, you will be expected to build strong teams, motivate and inspire people to do more than they thought they could, maintain high standards in tough times, look for and advance high-potential talent, bring diverse perspectives to the table, develop staff you inherited as well as hired, and create an inclusive environment where everyone can be engaged and successful.

- **Create Your Personal Brand**: The concept of creating a brand for an individual employee versus one for a product or service is still relatively new, but is rapidly gaining importance for a career. Your Personal Brand describes who you are, what you do, and how you bring value to the company. Everyone has a brand of some sort that reflects the reputation her or she has in the company. Until recently, people didn't always know their brand or reputation, nor did they think to actively manage it as part of their complete professional package. I strongly encourage my clients to create and proactively maintain a Personal Brand Statement that accurately reflects how they want to be perceived, that sells them as the product, and that makes them attractive to customers (potential mentors, sponsors, and future bosses).

Despite the seeming scarcity of resources and opportunities, companies still need good talent, and the strongest performers are still getting ahead. This is a time to step up and do things beyond what is required for your job. Differentiate yourself from your peers and colleagues, as you want be considered someone who is among the best. Find the areas in your business that are growing and continuously sharpen your skill set and add to your toolbox in ways that make you relevant there.

Chapter 2
Self-Coaching and Development Assignment:

Creating Your Personal Brand Statement

This assignment is designed to help you create a compelling, concise, memorable one-sentence Personal Brand Statement that describes who you are, what you do, and how you add value to your company, firm, organization, hospital, university, elementary school, police department, government agency, armed service branch, world—yet it should be simple enough for your neighbors and even children to understand it. You will use your Personal Brand Statement constantly to give people a snapshot of who you are.

What Is a Personal Brand Statement?

A Personal Brand Statement:

- **Communicates who you are:** your vision, your values, your background, what's important to you, why you do what you do

- **Describes what you're known for:** Your academic training, your field of endeavor, your expertise and experience, your body of work

- **Reflects your hallway reputation:** the first thing people say about you when your name comes up in conversation

- **Positions and differentiates you.** In order to get to the top, you must "pop out of the pile," according to Jack Welch, legendary retired CEO of the General Electric Company. How do you distinguish yourself from your peers and competitors? What makes you a standout candidate in a crowd of contenders?

- **Clarifies the value you add:** what you specifically bring to your organization that makes it a better place, drives the business forward, brings in more customers, makes customers more satisfied, makes employees more engaged, impacts the bottom line, is a best practice in your industry

Here are some statements I heard executives use recently to describe how they add value:

- ✓ "I convince people to buy our product despite its relative high cost."

- ✓ "I help the company understand what the customer wants and needs."

- ✓ "I help people achieve the career success they desire."

- ✓ "I help the company "see around corners" to anticipate the next big thing."

A Personal Brand Statement is not your job title or job description; nor is it an accounting of your day-to-day activities, your goals, or your objectives. It is essentially your mission statement—for "Company YOU." Think of yourself as a product that must be attractive enough to catch the attention of potential buyers (your bosses) and a better value proposition than the competition (the other candidates for the position) even if you are more expensive.

Here are a few examples of Personal Brand Statements for

illustrative purposes only. Your statement should be crafted to fit you specifically.

- ✓ *"I make a difference in the world by really connecting with the people who work with me, helping them understand the inextricable link between their personal authenticity and professional value, and then recognizing and confronting what's been holding them back so that we win as a team." (business team leader)*

- ✓ *"With a passion for wine and a natural, open approach, I inspire others to appreciate the pleasure of good wines in a fun way." (wine tasting host)*

- ✓ *"Through my natural enthusiasm and my empathy for others, I inspire research and development professionals to develop innovative products in biotechnology." (biotech manager)*

- ✓ *"I use my 25 years of experience in and passion for marketing to help senior marketing executives in large organizations succeed by increasing the way marketing is valued by the organization". (marketing trainer)*

- ✓ *"Through my intuition and genuine concern for and interest in others, I build long-lasting, fruitful relationships with my team, my business partners, and clients to drive consistent, recurring revenue for my company." (business owner)*

Crafting Your Personal Brand Statement

Before you begin writing your Personal Brand Statement, you might find it helpful to reflect on core elements that make you who you are and determine why you do what you do. Let's start with your vision. Whether or not you're conscious of it, you have some sort of vision that guides your activities, both long-term and short-term. I think of vision as the guiding theme of both our personal and professional lives. It is a vivid description of the future—a picture—that focuses our efforts and directs our decisions, plans, and actions throughout our lives.

All savvy, successful companies have spent time and effort honing their vision statements because they know the power of having a large group of people aligned around the same guiding theme. Your vision reflects your values and your philosophy and establishes what's important to you. Your vision can be lofty and difficult, if not impossible, to achieve. And that's okay, because your vision is a long-term goal that you are always striving to reach. Even if you never reach the goal, what you achieve along the journey is well worth it. An example of a lofty vision might be, "I will use my skills, talents, and resources to make sure there are no starving children in the world." You may not feed all the starving children in the world in your lifetime, but you will make a huge difference in the lives of the children you *are* able to feed along the way.

Listing Your Values and Creating a Vision Statement

Take out a sheet of paper and draw two columns. In the first column, list your core values. In the second column, write your Vision Statement. Don't worry if you miss a couple of values; you can add them later. The same goes for your Vision Statement: write down a good first draft and allow yourself the option of editing it later as things become clearer.

Creating Your Mission Statement

Which Words Best Express Your Values?

Here are some to get you thinking as you create your own list:

honesty

courage

forgiveness

optimism

sharing

love

understanding

integrity

respect

discipline

empathy

mutual respect

loyalty

communication

sharing

tolerance

hard work

flexibility

independent

logical

family-focused

environmentally conscious

Now that you've clarified your values and your vision for your future, it's time to create a mission statement for "Company YOU." Typically, an organization's Mission Statement describes its purpose; why it exists. It makes the Vision Statement more concrete and actionable. While you may have the same vision for 20 or more years, your Mission Statement will change much more frequently. At different stages of your life, the way you achieve your vision may take different forms, and your Mission Statement will reflect that. So your Vision Statement is more long-term, and your Mission Statement is more short-term, spanning, say, three to five years. Both should reflect both your personal and your professional lives.

Let's look at some examples of a Mission Statement based on the Vision Statement about saving starving children:

Vision Statement	Mission Statement
"I will use my skills, talents, and resources to make sure there are no starving children in the world."	I will use my degree in pediatric medicine to better understand the nutritional needs of young children. I will work for a company that creates and sells healthy food for children in a role that, among other responsibilities, allows me to educate families on how best to provide nutritious meals and encourage healthy snack choices, even in reduced financial circumstances. I will influence my company to donate food to hungry children here in the United States and serve as a liaison. I will work with and then start my own non-profit organization that raises money to feed the healthiest food possible to starving children in the United States, whose needs are often forgotten.

Now it's your turn. Create two new side-by-side columns and, as in the example above, write your Vision Statement in the left column and your Mission Statement in the right column. Copy your vision statement into the left column and create a new mission statement for the right column.

Creating Your Personal Brand Statement

Now that you've clarified your values, your vision, and your mission, you're ready to craft your Personal Brand Statement: a compelling, concise, memorable, one-sentence description of who you are, what you do, and how you add value both personally and professionally.

- Review your list of your values, your Vision Statement, and your Mission Statement.

- Now take out a sheet of paper and write down the first sentence that comes to mind as a possible Personal Brand Statement. Don't worry about how long it is, how it sounds, or how it reads just yet. Walk away from it for a day or two.

- Go back to your draft Personal Brand Statement and review it again. Does it convey what is really important to you and why you do what you do? Make any edits you think are appropriate, spending no more than 30 to 60 minutes on it. Again, walk away from it for a day or two.

- Read your Personal Brand Statement this time to make sure it conveys how you add value to your company. Again, make any edits you think are appropriate, spending no more than 30 to 60 minutes on it. Share it with two or three trusted members of your network and get their feedback. Write down everything they say. Walk away from your Personal Brand Statement and the feedback for two or three days. Then make any revisions you think are appropriate.

- Now collect five recent announcements from your office about people who were promoted to a position at least one or two levels above yours. Try to find at least one or two announcements about colleagues you know and respect. Find an additional one or two about people retiring from the company at any level above your level.

- Review each announcement and write down the Personal Brand Statements for each executive, including what's important to him, why she does what she does, how she adds value to the company, and why he is being promoted. Also note for the retirees the legacy they leave behind.

- What messages can you take away from the announcements in terms of what is important and valued in your company's culture? Which words are used consistently for the most successful people?

- How might these insights change the approach you have taken to your Personal Brand Statement? Are you using your company's language of success? Review and revise your statement as appropriate. Again, practice using it with both people who know you as well as strangers you meet in the grocery store, at the dry cleaner, and at your son's football or Little League game. Note their reactions and the questions they ask.

- Finally, share your draft Personal Brand Statement with someone in your network who is a brand manager for a product or service. Ask him or her to review it and provide feedback on how well it reflects and sells you. Note the feedback and again make revisions and refinements as necessary.

- Use your refined Personal Brand Statement as often and in as many ways as possible. For example, consider putting it in your e-mail signature. Include it in your elevator speech. Put it at the top of your resume after your contact information. Use it when you meet new people and they ask you what you do. Include it in your Facebook, LinkedIn, and Twitter profiles. The more you use it, the easier it will become to use—and each time you use it will increase brand awareness of Company YOU.

- Review your Personal Brand Statement two to three times a year (and after every job change or significant experience) and update it as appropriate. Be sure to periodically check announcements of senior-level promotions to ensure that your Personal Brand Statement continues to reflect the current language used to describe successful, upwardly-mobile executives in your company.

PART II

Some Important and Often Unwritten Rules

CHAPTER 3:
Rule #1 – There Is a Game Being Played, Whether You Know It or Not

This rule is often difficult for some people to understand and accept as they begin their careers in corporate life. Corporate life is a game, and the serious players are in it to win power, prestige, and perks. It is your choice whether to acknowledge and play the game or not.

- **The game is played according to military and sports models because most of the players at the top are men and these are the models they know.** The military model teaches ideas like strategy, offense and defense, good guys and bad guys, winning and losing, and chain of command— with officers taking care of their troops and the troops obedient to and executing their officers' commands. The sports model follows all of these principles, but it stresses competition and strong coaching to develop the abilities of the players to win as a team.

  In American culture, most boys start competing in team sports at an early age. As young men they may also spend some time in military training. So they often have an advantage over women when it comes to learning the rules of the game early.

- **The game is about winning and losing.** There is no middle ground in the corporate game. You either get the job and win, or you are not selected and lose. Similarly, you either get the business and win, or your competitor gets it and you lose. A mediocre performance will not be graded as a winning performance. This may be difficult for some women to grasp who come into the workplace more familiar with the family model, where the mother seeks to deal with everyone evenhandedly and to produce a win/win outcome for all. Women involved in competitive sports will understand this win/lose concept and it will serve them quite well in the work environment.

- **The game is about people and relationships.** When you understand this rule, you will work constantly to make connections, to establish relationships, and to manage these relationships. We call this "networking," but the term doesn't begin to suggest how much time, effort, and attention it takes to build strong connections and mutually beneficial relationships with people who think well of you and are willing to put themselves out for you.

- **How the game is played reflects the company culture.** Every company has a culture; some are more distinct than others. The person at the top defines the company culture—how things are done, how people speak and communicate, the behaviors that are acceptable and not acceptable. In order to be successful in corporate life, you must accurately read the environment you're in. You must know how things work and who the key people are. You must be able to work within the system and do so consistently and well.

- **The game demands loyalty and sacrifice.** One of the unwritten rules in corporate America is that the closer you get to the top, the more willing you are to eat, sleep, and breathe "the company," to be on call 24 hours a day, seven days a week. The loyalty cuts both ways: the corporate soldiers follow their commander and the commander takes care of the soldiers. And everyone makes personal sacrifices. If you get to the point where you are unwilling to make further sacrifices, then you need to be comfortable staying at your present level, because each successive level will demand additional sacrifices.

- **The game requires team players.** This rule means that you must be able to lead when necessary and follow when necessary. Leadership moves around depending on the needs of the project. The team comes first. The team's needs, issues, and concerns supersede the needs, issues, and concerns of the individual. So you must be prepared to be flexible, to play whatever role is required of you by the team at any given point in time.

    There are some other key principles associated with being a team player. It is much more than simply being cooperative and willing. First, as a senior leader, you are accountable for your team. Whatever happens, good or bad, the responsibility rests with you. And while you may "take the hit" when something goes wrong, you usually share the glory when something goes well. You say, "We did it," not "I did it."

- **You must be "on your game" at all times.** Being in the game is like being pregnant: you either are, or you aren't. There is virtually no moment in the day when you can present yourself as anything other than competent, dedicated, and in command of yourself. How you dress in the morning, greet your coworkers, follow through on projects, gather and use information, make connections, create solutions—all these are essential pieces of your game plan for advancement. There is little room for miscalculation, and if you do trip up, you must act immediately to dispel the bad impression and replace it with a good impression by demonstrating performance, execution, and results.

- The game is often more challenging for women and people of color. Indeed, the game is initially more difficult for *anyone* who has little experience with the military and sports models that inspire the cultures of corporate America and their white male colleagues. Women have additional trade-offs to make having to do with motherhood and running their households. People of color have to deal with issues of their "otherness." Where their white middle-class colleagues may have learned something about the business world at the family dinner table, African American, Latino/Hispanic, and Asian employees may not have had even that small degree of preparation.

- **The game is not fair.** Remember this rule when you lose an opportunity for advancement to someone who is benefiting from a stronger relationship with the potential boss than you have, or someone who is not (either by choice or biological impossibility) going to become pregnant, or someone who has no responsibilities that would interfere with taking that plum job in Paris. The game is what it is, but *the choices are always yours.*

CHAPTER 4:
Rule #2 - The Person at the
Top Makes the Rules

The rules of the game and the company culture flow from the person at the top of the pyramid. In most companies, it's the CEO who makes the rules and decides how the game is played, picks the key players for his team, clarifies acceptable and unacceptable behavior for winning, and defines the rewards and consequences for adhering to or breaking the rules. Needless to say, all of this changes each time there is a new CEO: suddenly there are new rules, and everyone in the organization has to adapt and adjust. Your knowledge of the unwritten rules will be your lifejacket in any sea change in the company power structure.

You make the rules for your department. That is the power given to you by your role as the head of the department, and you are expected to use it and use it wisely. As a member of management and thus the CEO's team, your job is to follow the CEO's rules while making a few of your own for your department. As a department head, for example, you are expected to know and describe how your team wins, identify acceptable and unacceptable behaviors for getting there, and administer rewards and consequences for adhering to or breaking the rules. You are essentially the CEO of your department. Failing to play your role appropriately as the department head will create a vacuum someone else will fill, taking your power even if they don't officially take your position. While you may continue to be the formal leader according to the organization chart, that person will become the real, albeit informal, leader of the department. Worse yet, you will have signaled to all that you are inept at playing the game. Men often say that the reason they don't like working for women is that women "just don't get it." What they're really saying is that women are often dismal at playing the game and therefore not helpful to them and their career success. So, as a woman in charge of a project or department, make the rules and enforce them. No one, male or female, should ever willingly relinquish power to another player in the game without a vigorous fight.

Chapter 5:
Rule #3 - The Boss (Almost) Always Wins and Is Absolutely Critical to Your Career Success

Pick your boss carefully. The most successful people pick their bosses well in advance—perhaps two or three moves in advance. They look at their career plan and decide what their next position needs to be to achieve their ultimate goal. They find out who manages that position, and then use their network to bring themselves to the attention of that potential boss. People who allow the organization to decide their career path for them are significantly less likely to achieve the career success they desire.

My advice to you is to think at least two moves ahead. For each move, you want a position with a boss who can help you gain the skills and exposure you'll need for the job you'll want after that. This is called *strategic career management*. In addition:

- **Work on things that matter.** Your job is to produce the results your boss needs. So work on things that are important to your boss and to your boss's boss. Suppose you propose a project that you think will benefit the company and your reputation. If your boss doesn't think it's important, you have to set that project aside and work on what matters most to him or her. That's the only way to get the time, attention, exposure, resources, and recognition you need for career success. As one executive explained to me, "Don't commit too much time to things 'off the beaten trail'—work on things that matter."

- **Get the job done at all costs—no excuses.** Your boss gives you a project on the assumption that you will get it done. The company is well aware you may have to sacrifice something in order to make it happen. In fact, the more sacrifice required, the more of a test it is, because virtually no one gets to the top without making a series of sacrifices throughout his or her career. If you are unprepared to make sacrifices at lower levels in the company, the company will likely conclude that there's no point promoting you to higher levels, since the sacrifices required there are even greater. The way the game is played, huge sacrifice reaps huge rewards. Your CEO knows, better than anyone else in the company, what it means to have to work nights, weekends, and holidays. The company is essentially saying: "This project is important to our business, and we have given it to you, someone we trust to get it done on time and on budget—and without whining." Consistently follow through on your commitments, because no excuses are ever really acceptable.

- **Always make your boss look good.** It helps to think of your boss as your #1 customer. Never, by anything you say or fail to say, cause your boss to lose face. You may be tempted at times to speak out when it looks as though your boss will take all the credit for something you did. Resist the urge. In most cases, your colleagues know exactly who is doing what, and eventually you will get the credit you deserve. (Note: If you find yourself hardly ever getting the credit you deserve, you may not be promoting yourself effectively.) Your ultimate goal is to become one of your boss's trusted go-to people. These are the people who get the best assignments, the most exposure and visibility to potential sponsors, the best performance ratings, and the first pick of plum jobs.

- **Always have a solution ready for any problem you present to your boss.** Before you take a problem to your boss, either fix it or be ready to offer a fix for it. Show that you are capable, accountable, and responsible for your own work. If you cannot solve problems, you'll never go above middle management.

- **Never argue aggressively with your boss.** You will never look good contradicting your boss in front of others, and your career ultimately will not survive it. You'll be viewed as disloyal, as someone who doesn't know how to play the game. If you're better informed on the matter under discussion and your boss is wrong, provide the correct information in private or pass a note during the meeting. The only time to argue aggressively is *in support of your boss.*

- **Never whine, and *never, ever* cry.** If you whine, you set yourself apart from the people who are going on to higher levels. They are willing to make the sacrifices without whining; you must be, too. Remember, it is a game and the game is not always fair. As a woman in your organization, you may find yourself having to disprove the assumption of your male colleagues that you can't handle the pressure; that you're not tough enough. So, no whining and no crying. Both will weaken your image, and it will take months, maybe years, to erase the bad impression they make.

- **Have a cheerful, can-do attitude.** It's great to be a person with a reputation for getting it done. But people will like you even better if you're cheerful about it, if you're positive and proactive. They'll have no hesitation about coming to you for help in getting difficult things accomplished. Your can-do attitude is a signal that you are a team player and ready to handle whatever they throw at you. As such, you will be sought after and you will get ahead.

- **The boss (almost) always wins.** All the rules above have to do with building a good relationship with your boss. How you manage that relationship is critical to your career because your boss has the power to kill your career. But a boss who is appreciative of your loyalty and commitment will be your supporter and will grant you important insider status. That you manage the relationship well will add to your good reputation in the company. If your boss is so difficult that you can't build a good relationship, then it's time to move on, because *the boss always wins.*

Brenda's Story: The Cost of Criticizing the Boss

Brenda was as an Executive Vice President leading a major business unit in her company. She didn't have much respect for her boss, and she knew most of his other direct reports had similar views. Those views somehow reached the CEO, who hired a consultant to coach Brenda's boss.

The consultant asked Brenda and her peers to provide feedback about her boss, which he then provided to her boss as anonymous feedback. Most of it was pretty negative. The consultant arranged an offsite "group learning event" so her boss could "hear concerns more directly and have a conversation about how he could change key behaviors and perceptions."

During the session, Brenda was determined to follow her instincts and, as she put it, "keep my mouth shut." But, she recalls, "after much prodding from the consultant, I shared my concerns and impressions with my manager. No one else did. Everyone else was completely quiet." The meeting finally ended early when none of the others shared their feelings. Unfortunately, by that time, the damage to Brenda had been done. Despite just about everyone else having similar feelings, Brenda was the only person who verbalized them in public.

Brenda quickly realized she had broken almost every unwritten rule regarding the boss-direct report relationship. She had failed to make her boss look good and, most critically, she had neglected to build and maintain a strong positive relationship with her boss despite how she felt about him.

Brenda admits candidly that her relationship with that boss never recovered from that incident. She is convinced he used every opportunity from then on to undermine and discredit her. "The lesson I learned is that no matter how unhappy you are or how legitimate your complaints may be, keep your criticisms of your boss to yourself, particularly when you lack a strong, positive relationship."

Lesson learned: The boss always wins.

CHAPTER 6:
Rule #4 – Exposure, Visibility and Strategic Networking are Career Accelerators

Without exposure and visibility, your outstanding work has little impact on your career success. The right people need to know how good you are if you want sustained career success. Who are the right people? Anyone who could possibly help you make the career moves you have planned, including potential bosses, mentors, and sponsors. Exposure is the means by which you make yourself and your work known and build a good reputation throughout your company and beyond. It's your primary means of attracting a mentor and a sponsor—and the mechanism for attracting the next boss you want. If you're getting no exposure to your boss, his or her boss and peers, and people at least two levels above you, you are not going to move up. It's as simple as that. Every day presents opportunities for getting exposure: meetings, committees, task forces, special projects, town hall meetings, conference calls, and casual meetings in the hallway, elevator, and at the water cooler. Recognize and act on these opportunities by being well prepared. Your goal is to use effective self-promotion to market yourself during exposure opportunities. Here are some issues to consider:

- Do you have a compelling, one-sentence description of what you do and how that adds value to the company (your Personal Brand Statement.) Have you checked to see who is attending the meeting whom you might want to meet and connect with?

- How might you start a conversation with that person?

- Is someone else attending the meeting who might introduce the two of you?

- How else might you strategically network during the meeting to meet people you would not otherwise have access to?

It's important to note that effective self-promotion requires a fine balance between humility and assertiveness, keeping in mind your company's culture around getting ahead at the expense of others. Many people mistakenly believe their work will speak for itself. That belief is a recipe for disaster. Not only will your work *not* speak for itself, but if you don't take credit for it, someone else likely will. Asian and Hispanic/Latino employees, whose cultures reinforce modesty, often have difficulty promoting and marketing themselves effectively, which can be a major barrier to their success. Effective marketing and self-promotion are critical career accelerators. Learn how to do them well.

Remember: relationships make the world go 'round. Networking is the art and science of making connections and building relationships. In every organization, things get done primarily based on relationships. She or he who has more relationships, and thus the bigger network, essentially has more power and resources. So you must make connections and build your network as a critical resource that's always ready and available to you when you need it. I believe networking is such a force multiplier that I recommend everyone devote at least 5% of their work week to networking.

Networking requires a consistent, conscious effort to nurture and maintain each relationship. The good news is that we network all the time, both personally and professionally, even if we don't think of it as networking. We network when we stay in touch with relatives and remember their birthdays and special occasions. We network when we strike up a conversation with a stranger and end up exchanging contact information. We network when we send out holiday cards. We network when we ask colleagues if they had a nice weekend or a good vacation. We network when we congratulate a colleague on a promotion. We network when spending time chatting with coworkers before a meeting. We network when we go to a work-related social event and meet at least one person we didn't know or reconnect with someone. We network when we relax on the weekend with friends, family, or colleagues. Consciously or unconsciously, we network all the time. Getting to the top and staying there entails networking strategically and with a purpose.

Fortunately, if you keep making small efforts consistently over time, it's possible to nurture and build many many connections. There is an art to connecting with others. A lot of it has to do with finding interests you have in common. Look at the whole person as you search for common interests: professional activities, community work, philanthropic activities, common friends and acquaintances, personal interests and hobbies, children, and sports. The smallest detail—say, a book the person is carrying—can provide a clue about common interests and an opening for a friendly exchange. From there, in later exchanges, you can learn more about the person's interests, as you reveal yours. You are now in each other's constellation of friends (even if distant friends) and supporters. You might exchange information and favors, personal or professional, collecting the "chits" you may each cash in later. Once firmly established in your network, these are the people you can go to for information, whom you can count on to put in a good word for you, who will give you honest feedback on your reputation, and a heads-up when things are going awry. Your network is a living, breathing resource that needs continuous nourishment. Above all, be genuine in reaching out. Your interest in others needs to be sincere, otherwise you will be dismissed as merely manipulative.

Mariko's Story: "Networking Works!"

Mariko, a Vice President in a large consumer goods company, had had a stellar career that had outpaced 90% of her peers' from the time she joined the company straight out of business school to her promotion to VP level. But once there, she observed that the competition for jobs at the Senior Vice President level was quite fierce, and that the rapid movement of some people's careers had begun to slow down—including, unfortunately, her own.

Since she continued to achieve superior results and received outstanding performance ratings, she was at a loss to understand what was happening to her career. At first she first thought she was imagining things, but when her colleague Al, who'd become a VP after her, was promoted to SVP, she began to worry that her career slowdown might be related to the fact that she was a woman and Asian. She decided to ask her mentor about it.

When Mariko had lunch with her mentor the following week, they discussed the situation and, after a careful analysis, decided that it definitely was not a performance issue, nor was it a race or gender issue—at least not directly. Mariko's mentor mentioned something that really struck her. Apparently, every Friday after work, a group of people from the office went to the restaurant next door for Happy Hour to have a couple of drinks and a bite to eat. While different people stopped by on different Fridays, there was a core group of people who showed up every week, and some of the fastest-moving people in the company were in that group... including Al! They used that time to get caught up on the latest "intelligence" about what was going on in the company. They sometimes knew things weeks ahead of everyone else.

Mariko's mentor asked her if she'd ever been invited to attend. She told him she had but had declined because "after a long, tough week, I just want to get home to my family." Her mentor told her that spending those few hours on Friday evening would do more for her career than all the extra hours she put in every week and on the weekends. Mariko decided to see if he was right.

For five of the next six weeks, Mariko attended the Happy Hour sessions and became a "regular." As she says, "I can honestly say, with no exaggeration, that before I started attending those Happy Hour sessions, I was clueless about what was really going on in my company."

Mariko learned two critical lessons: knowledge is power, and a good network is an invaluable source of knowledge. Once Mariko was an active member in the network, she heard about several positions that were perfect next jobs for her. Based on the information she gained at the Happy Hour sessions, she was able to position herself appropriately and was ultimately promoted to Senior Vice President in a very short period of time. Mariko is now a dedicated networker and makes time for it in her schedule. As she says, "networking works!"

CHAPTER 6
Self-Coaching and
Development Assignment:

Creating a Visibility and Exposure Plan

This assignment is designed to help you develop a six-month Exposure and Visibility Plan to identify, prepare for, and manage your opportunities for exposure and visibility so that you may attract a great opportunity, mentor, sponsor, and/or next boss.

1. Let's begin by focusing on your upcoming visibility and exposure opportunities and how you want to use them. How can you best maximize your exposure opportunities so that you can achieve the success you desire and deserve? Can you use your visibility and exposure opportunities to:

    - Gain a mentor?

    - Gain a sponsor (e.g., your boss' boss)?

    - Find your next boss?

    - Build/maintain your network?

    - Market your Personal Brand?

    - Enhance your hallway reputation?

    - Address your developmental opportunities?

    - Achieve your career goals?

Your responses to the two questions below will help you identify the strategic purpose of your networking:

- *What* do you want to accomplish during the next six months that will be facilitated by conscious, purposeful networking?

- *Who* will you need to network with to accomplish your goal?

Jot down your answers on a sheet of paper.

2. Next, take out your calendar and look for all the meetings and events you have scheduled both personally and professionally for the next six months where you can network with a purpose. Make a complete list of them by month.

3. Highlight the meetings and events which leaders two or more levels above you will attend, particularly if you're on the agenda as a presenter. Those are prime visibility and exposure opportunities and should be planned for and executed accordingly.

4. Now highlight the meetings the people you listed in #1 above will attend. Focus on the meetings where both groups overlap. Those have highest priority for maximizing visibility and exposure.

5. Develop a specific, detailed plan for the first upcoming meeting.

- Identify the 2 to 3 people you will make your best effort to meet.

- Do your homework on each of those individuals. Identify the connection points between you. Attended same college? Both worked in manufacturing in your early careers? Both have sons who play hockey? Die-hard Red Sox fans?

- Clarify in your mind what you want from this encounter. If this is the early stage of your relationship, I would suggest your goal might be to make enough of a connection to warrant a follow-up e-mail and/or phone call.

- Refresh and practice your Personal Brand Statement and elevator speech. Keep practicing until they both sound smooth and natural in conversation.

- Now practice your entry. As you walk up to each person, what will you say as you introduce yourself and shake his or her hand? What will you say next? Practice various ways of weaving what you want to say into the conversation.

- Finally, think about your exit. How will you smoothly leave this individual with a good impression after about 2 to 3 minutes of conversation?

6. Move on to the next person and develop a similar detailed plan. The more you do this the easier it becomes and, before you know it, strategic networking that pays huge dividends will become a natural part of your routine.

CHAPTER 7:
Rule #5 - Your Hallway Reputation Precedes You, So Make Sure It's a Competitive Advantage

Your hallway reputation is what is said about you when, for example, a potential boss asks someone in his or her network about you. In as few as two to three sentences, your hallway reputation can be conveyed: "She's reliable… he has good judgment… she gets results" and so on. What people say about you gets around. That's why it's important to use your large network of active supportive contacts both inside and outside the company to manage your reputation.

In building your hallway reputation, you want to be known, first of all, as someone who gets results, consistently performing above expectations. In addition:

- You want to be known for your expertise and credibility: that you can be trusted to use your knowledge and skills to deliver what you promise, on time and on budget.

- You want to be known for your loyalty and commitment, as someone who lives according to the core values of the company, and as someone who "does the right thing" consistently with honesty and integrity.

- You want to be known as someone who embraces change, who can adapt to innovations and initiatives, reorganizations and restructurings—including keeping up with and embracing technology.

Immediately take steps to counter any negative opinion. Your strong, positive hallway reputation is a precious commodity. As soon as you hear that something unfavorable is being said about you, make a plan to restore your good hallway reputation.

Find out the source and the context of the poor report. Gather data and information to support your position and use your network to explain your position and offer another more positive perspective. Above all, do not leave the bad opinion out there to snowball. Let nothing and no one adversely impact your hallway reputation without trying to mitigate or dispel the negative impression. Often people form opinions with few facts. Make the facts known to your network and ask them to dispel any misperceptions when they hear them. Replace the negative talk with good news about your team's recent accomplishments.

Finally, keep track of your hallway reputation. At least three times a year, survey different members of your network to find out what's being said about you. And then act accordingly: reinforce your good hallway reputation, take steps to correct misperceptions, and eliminate any behaviors that lead to negative impressions.

CHAPTER 8:
Rule #6 - You Need a Sponsor to Pull You Up to Higher Levels

A sponsor is someone who respects your work, believes that you can contribute value at the next level, and is powerful enough to pull you up through the system. I think of two basic types of sponsorship: direct and indirect. A direct sponsor is someone who can actually give you the job; that is, the person with the open position to fill. An indirect sponsor is someone who can influence the leader with the open position to consider you as a candidate. Never underestimate the power of an indirect sponsor. If the relationship is strong enough, a sponsor has been known to accept the candidate sight unseen on the strength of a recommendation by an indirect sponsor.

Your direct sponsor generally needs to be two or more levels above your level in order to give you a promotion. Therefore, to become your boss's peer at the next level, you need a sponsor with direct reports at that level. In most organizations, that means someone at least two levels above you. The same is true for your direct sponsorship of someone. You can directly sponsor someone for open positions that report to you. My guess is you do not have any positions reporting to you that are also on your same level. Therefore, you cannot directly sponsor any of your direct reports to a position at your level. Only someone at your boss's level can do that.

Indirect sponsorship works a little differently because you

play more of an advocate role. You may advocate for someone who is below you, a peer, or even above you. You are essentially recommending that individual for consideration by the person who has the open position. I repeat, never underestimate the power of an indirect sponsor—including when that indirect sponsor is you. If the sponsor trusts your judgment, your recommendation carries a lot of weight and typically ensures that the candidate receives at least a courtesy interview.

You may not always know who sponsored you for a particular position. It may be someone who knows of you by reputation and has seen your work but never met you. In most cases, however, your potential sponsor will speak with you about the open position before recommending you to ensure you are in fact interested in the role. Have you ever had a friend or colleague call or email to tell you to expect a call from someone who is looking to fill a position because he gave her your name? You were just sponsored for a job.

Long before you're aware that a potential sponsor is considering you, he or she will have weighed a number of factors to determine your eligibility. Your consistently outstanding performance is the first criterion. A sponsor is attracted to success, and there's no better success indicator than results that exceed expectations. That is the WHAT of the equation.

A sponsor will also care about HOW you achieved those results—your behaviors and leadership. Did you motivate and inspire your team to success, or did you bully them to the finish line? Did you share the credit or take it all for yourself? Did you use assignments as opportunities to grow and develop your team?

Your sponsor will also consider your relationships and reputation; that is, what is your reputation among your direct reports, peers, colleagues, and HR? Your reputation will be a direct reflection of your relationships with them. What kinds of relationships do you have with senior leaders, including your mentor(s) and your sponsor's peers? What your boss says about you will be considered quite carefully, particularly the consistency between what she says about you and the performance rating, merit increase, and bonus she gave you. And finally, your personality, interpersonal skills, and executive presence will give your sponsor a sense of how well you'll fit in. A candidate who will easily fit in generally trumps the candidate whose fit is uncertain.

When and where does a sponsor do her work? There are both formal and informal occasions when a leader performs the role of sponsor. The most formal occasion is the succession planning meeting, where leaders and HR meet to review current and potential open positions and candidates ready, available, and appropriate to fill them. The sponsor's role during that meeting is to present a compelling case for people he thinks would be strong candidates for a particular role and to mitigate any negative perceptions others in the room may mention. Both direct and indirect sponsors can play an influential advocate role during this meeting. Sponsors will put forward only the strongest candidates, in order to avoid developing a reputation for promoting mediocre talent.

Whenever there is a discussion about a promotion or job change, sponsors may engage in more informal conversations about recommended candidates. Before a promotion, most candidates are vetted by a number of people they have worked for and with, including former bosses. Each of those persons, and anyone providing a strong, positive recommendation, is essentially serving as an indirect sponsor.

In the sponsorship process, you can control the outcome to the extent that you can ensure that your performance is outstanding and that you have an excellent brand and hallway reputation. The rest of the process takes place essentially behind closed doors and is out of your control. You may receive candid feedback on what was actually said about you if you have a mentor or trusted member of your network who participated in the discussion; otherwise, I have found people generally avoid the topic.

I have been asked whether people can cultivate a sponsor or solicit sponsorship or whether they must wait until someone decides to sponsor them. The answer to that question depends on the four critical factors I described above—your performance, reputation, personal brand, and relationships. Cultivating and soliciting sponsorship can be quite successful if at least three of the four critical factors are extremely strong, you approach it using your very best interpersonal savvy, and look as though you are a good fit. During the solicitation process you are essentially selling yourself to the potential sponsor, and the critical factors are your value proposition. When the sponsor does his homework to check on you (and he definitely will), what he hears must make him completely comfortable putting his reputation on the line for you. And if you get the job, for the entire time you are in that position, you must continue to do outstanding work so your sponsor thinks he was a pretty smart guy recommending you.

For women and people of color, or expatriates from other countries, it is likely that your sponsor will be someone with a different background, ethnicity, and/or gender; someone who you may feel less comfortable with for any number of reasons. As you network to attract a mentor, sponsor, or next boss, force yourself to move out of your comfort zone and build relationships with people at higher levels who are quite unlike you. Find ways to connect and make them comfortable with you. The rewards for doing so are immeasurable.

CHAPTER 8
Self-Coaching and Development Assignment:

Past and Future Sponsors

This assignment is designed to help you identify past and future sponsors for the career trajectory you desire.

1. Think about the last three job changes you made (including, let's hope, a promotion). For each job, think back to who had to say yes in order for you to get the job. That person was most probably your sponsor. On a sheet of paper, jot down those names as past sponsors.

2. Think about the next two jobs you want. Who would have to say yes for you to be selected? Jot down the jobs you want and the names of direct sponsors for each.

3. Who might influence those direct sponsors to say yes? They would be indirect sponsors. Jot down those names and list them under indirect sponsors for each job.

4. Think about the kinds of relationships you have with both the direct and indirect sponsors for your next two preferred jobs. On a scale of 1 to 5, (5 being the highest), how would you rate your relationship with them at this point?

5. How could you cultivate or improve those relationships and bring yourself to their attention? What could you say to differentiate and communicate your value to them?

Jot down 2 or 3 ideas you have to build and maintain relationships with these people who are quite important to your career.

6. Now, execute your plan!

CHAPTER 9:
Rule #7 - Find Your "Best Fit" Mentors

A good mentor is someone who has committed to your career success and who therefore spends precious time coaching and developing you. The most effective mentoring relationships are win/win: both individuals give something and both receive something. The mentor benefits by being seen as someone who can recognize and develop winners. You benefit from having someone explain the rules of the game and provide feedback on how well you're playing it. Like sponsors, mentors are attracted to successful people. Hard work, results, and exposure help you attract them.

A wide variety of people can act as your mentor, including your parents and siblings. Typically, a mentor is a more experienced, seasoned, or senior executive who understands the rules of the game where you work. But as I've mentioned, I've seen and experienced good mentoring relationships with peers, colleagues, bosses and even direct reports or administrative assistants. Many times it's less about rank or title than about the knowledge and/ or skills the mentor has and is willing to share with you.

Mentors can be inside or outside your company and can select you or allow you to select them.

"Best-Fit Mentoring" relationships evolve from a natural affinity between two people. In this case, the relationship typically begins informally, generally after the two colleagues have met, worked together, and developed mutual respect. There's a shared belief that the time spent together is mutually beneficial. For example, the mentor may provide feedback on the best way to command a room when making an important presentation, and the mentee may teach the mentor how to set up and use a social media account.

There are a number of roles a mentor can play, and it's best to be clear about the desired role from the beginning. Your mentor may play the role of sounding board, coach, or confidante who explains the rules (including the unwritten ones) of the game. He or she will, ideally, provide candid, timely feedback (both positive and corrective) about how you're doing in your career, as well as early warning signals if something is going awry. As I mentioned in Chapter 2, I do not believe one mentor can meet all your development needs. You may require several mentors to address all of your developmental opportunities.

Before you actually begin working with your mentor, take the time to think about your career plan and the next two jobs you want.

- What knowledge, skills, experiences, expertise, know-how will you need to make you a competitve candidate for those jobs?

- Do you currently have what you need?

- Where are your biggest gaps?

- Which of those gaps can your current mentor help you with?

- Which gaps will require you to find other mentors to help close?

"Best-Fit Mentoring" occurs when there's a good match between the skill you need and the skill the mentor has to offer. Try to find best-fit mentors for your top three development needs. First, try to find someone you like and with whom you feel comfortable. Avoid anyone who will only give you praise or who will bury you with criticism. And by all means look for someone who is astute enough to correctly interpret how others react to you and forthcoming enough to give you honest feedback about your style or approach.

A best-fit mentor will assess your performance accurately and help you understand why it may fail to meet or exceed the expectations of your boss and upper management. She will also go to bat for you and push you to maximize your potential. Finally, this type of mentor is "in the loop" and can therefore alert you to new information, critical gossip, and rumors that may affect you as well as any changes—positive or negative—to your hallway reputation.

As you begin to work with your mentor, make him or her feel comfortable and make it easy to maintain a relationship with you:

- Take responsibility for setting up calls and meetings.

- Start small—don't ask for too much in the early stages of your relationship.

- Give back to your mentor by returning favors and being loyal.

- Have realistic expectations. If your mentor is senior and highly reputable, he or she is quite busy and probably mentoring several other people as well.

- Make the most of the time you have with your mentor and always arrive prepared for the meeting.

Finally, know when it's time to move on. Every mentoring relationship has a beginning and an end. When you've acquired the knowledge, insights, or skill you need from your mentor, your mentoring relationship transitions to a friendship in many instances.

People of color often complain about the lack of mentors, particularly at higher levels in the company, because they're wary of mentors who are different from themselves. When looking for a mentor, you will want to consider a myriad of possibilities: people who may come from very different backgrounds, places, cultures, education, and economic status. Rather than looking for similarities between you, look for the right match between your needs and the mentor's capabilities.

CHAPTER 9
Self-Coaching and
Development Assignment:

Finding Your Best-Fit Mentor

This assignment is designed to help you find a great match between your development needs and a mentor with the skills and expertise to effectively coach you for success.

1. Use the worksheet below to clarify the specific development needed to make you a viable candidate for your next two preferred jobs.

2. Identify 2 to 3 people who have a strong reputation for excellence in each of your development areas. First identify people who have already expressed an interest in helping you as a coach or mentor. Then move on to those with whom you have no current connection and determine who in your network might assist you in connecting with those potential mentors/coaches.

3. Develop and execute a plan of action for selling yourself as a protégée. Your Personal Brand Statement and your elevator speech should serve you well here. Your plan should also include how you will make the mentoring relationship mutually beneficial.

4. Execute your strategy to find best-fit mentors to address your specific development needs.

Finding Your Best-Fit Mentor

DEVELOPMENT AREA 1	POSSIBLE COACH/ MENTOR	SPECIFIC EXPERTISE OR SKILL PROVIDED
DEVELOPMENT AREA 2	POSSIBLE COACH/ MENTOR	SPECIFIC EXPERTISE OR SKILL PROVIDED
DEVELOPMENT AREA 3	POSSIBLE COACH/ MENTOR	SPECIFIC EXPERTISE OR SKILL PROVIDED

CHAPTER 10:
Rule #8 - You Need "Fit and Finish" Before Anyone Will Give You the Job

Doors will open to you when you look and behave like the people one or two levels above you. First there's *the fit*: you must dress the part so your visual image makes it easy for people at higher levels to see you working among them. Observe what is and what isn't acceptable in your company at the levels to which you aspire. Some companies have a narrow band of acceptability (no sandals, no sleeveless tops, no miniskirts, no facial hair). Dress to conform to your company's code of conduct, and when in doubt, err on the side of conservatism and quality.

Then there's *the finish*: your ability to communicate, behave, and fit into an environment without conscious thought; a kind of cultural fluency. The purpose of the interview for positions at higher levels is really to assess a candidate's fluency and fit in the environment. The more fluent you are in the culture of the desired job, the more comfortable with you your prospective boss will feel, increasing your likelihood of getting the job. Look and behave as though you belong in the position and the group. Some useful tips:

- Executive presence reflects your total package, including appearance, demeanor, personality, confidence, and attitude. Nearly every senior level position to which you aspire requires strong executive presence.

- Good manners, another aspect of finish, will take you

far. That means being courteous, showing good business etiquette, and having good table manners. Demonstrate your ease in social situations.

- Keep up with current events, books, movies and sports, so that you always have something to talk about.

Keep abreast of what's going on in the company. Know the stock price, key business issues and opportunities, new products, and other recent changes.

- While being a person of color makes it harder to visually fit in, the more you make people feel comfortable with you, the less they will notice your "otherness."

- Always leave a good impression. This is an important part of playing the game, because a bad impression, however minor, takes a long time to undo and can be a setback to your career.

Every interaction with senior leaders, whether it's in the conference room, the parking lot, or the supermarket, is an opportunity to demonstrate your fit and finish. When you are aiming for the top, executive presence, fit, and finish will take you across the finish line.

Elena's Story: Some Good Advice from the Boss

Elena, the most senior Latina female in an ultra-conservative manufacturing company, recently learned an invaluable lesson about image. Like many of her female colleagues, Elena struggles with work-family balance. She has three young children who have myriad school and after-school activities, most of which she misses. She also cares for her husband's aging parents, both of whom are showing early signs of dementia. There are days when the balancing act becomes overwhelming for her, especially given the early-morning and late- evening meetings and the travel expected of someone in her position.

Elena found herself feeling more and more guilty about all the school plays and soccer games she was missing and must have vocalized it too loudly or once too often with her colleagues, most of whom were male. Unbeknownst to her, her concerns got back to her boss, who took her out to lunch to "catch up on things."

During lunch her boss "got caught up" on all that was going on in Elena's life and talked a bit about what was going on in his life as well. To her surprise, he, too, was caring for an ailing mother with Alzheimer's, which he described as "quite stressful." She expressed her surprise at his calm demeanor at work when so much was going on at home. He reminded her that at the most senior levels in corporate America, you "can't let them see you sweat." No matter how tough it is, you must always "keep your cool." He told her people don't need to know your struggles and anxieties; only that you are on top of them and on top of your game. From that lunch on, Elena has kept her worries to herself and used friends outside of work as her support system. Lesson learned: Be on your game at all times and never let them see you sweat.

PART III

Everyone Gets into Trouble at Some Point

CHAPTER 11:
Avoiding and Overcoming Career Derailment

What exactly is career derailment? And does it mean the end of your career if it happens to you?

Career derailment occurs when your career stalls or goes into a downward spiral. Derailment typically follows failure to complete a series of assignments or to accomplish a series of tasks that meet the expectations of your manager or project leader. Derailment may also occur when your reputation becomes tarnished for whatever reason. In other instances, derailment may occur as a result of political maneuverings or a change in leadership.

The good news is that career derailment has happened at some point to almost everyone who has ever made it to the top. In fact, the issue is not so much the derailment as how you recognize and deal with it. The truth is, if you're taking appropriate risks and regularly operating outside your comfort zone, there's a strong chance that something at some point will not proceed as planned, and you find yourself in hot water.

Sometimes the derailment is unavoidable. Let's look at a common example.

> Jim Phillips, CEO of TopCorp, is nearing retirement. Jack and Russell are the two primary contenders to succeed him who are being given a year to prove themselves. Everyone knows one or the other will eventually get the position

and will likely form a kitchen cabinet of loyal followers to serve as direct reports.

Jane and Walter have ambitions to get to the top and become one of the new CEO's direct reports. But whose camp to join? Jane and Walter know that if you select the camp of the candidate who's ultimately tapped for the CEO position, you're in really good shape. But if you back the candidate who's not chosen, your career will derail.

Jane, fortunately, chooses the candidate who becomes the new CEO and has been given a great position in the new regime. Walter, on the other hand, is on the "losing side," and his candidate leaves the company soon after.

Does this mean the end of Walter's career? Absolutely not. Will Walter have considerable work to do to develop relationships with the new people in charge? Yes, he will, and has already begun to do so.

Common Career Derailers

Let's discuss some common derailers to avoid, why they'll get you into trouble, and how to get yourself out of trouble.

Sub-par Performance

- **Not making the numbers and then making excuses.** We've talked in previous chapters about how outstanding performance must be a given for continued career success. While you may make the occasional misstep, in general you must consistently deliver superior results year after year.

When you do miss your goal or target, you'll find yourself in trouble if you make excuses or blame others. The game is played with no excuses: If you find yourself saying, "I could have met my target if...", you are likely about to make an excuse. You must take accountability by owning up to your misstep and assuring your boss it won't happen again: "I blew it this time, but it will not happen again. Here is what is salvageable and what I will do next to fix it." Avoid at all costs blaming your team and "throwing them under the bus." As their leader and manager, it is your job to ensure they have everything they need for success. Their misstep is your misstep, and you must take accountability for it.

- **Making poor decisions or failing to make decisions.** In all likelihood, one of the key reasons for your misstep is making what your company considers to be a poor decision or no decision. As you rise into senior ranks, the problems you're expected to solve and the decisions you're expected to make become both more critical and more complex. Solving problems, making decisions, and leading and managing people are the essence of most senior roles in most organizations. If you are not an expert problem solver and decision maker, you will not reach the highest levels of your firm.

  Decision making is the final step in the problem-solving process and you can be good at one or the other, both or neither. Problem solving involves identifying the root causes of the problem, determining possible alternative solutions, and weighing the pros and cons of each possible solution. Decision making involves selecting the best option from among the various alternatives and then executing it. If your problem-solving/decision-making process is considered flawed, reflects poor judgment, or leads to an "avoidable mistake," it will trigger your derailment. Similarly, making no decision may also lead to derailment, as it is often considered a decision to maintain the status quo—again, unacceptable. Just know that it will be impossible to advance your career to the most senior levels with a reputation for poor problem solving or decision making.

- **Allowing others to set the agenda for your job.** At the most senior levels, you are expected to determine how best to make a significant contribution to the success of the company from where you sit. That means you are expected to set the agenda—identify the goals, targets, strategies, and tactics—for yourself and your team to win. And you must communicate your agenda up, down, and sideways in the organization with poise and confidence.

What happens if you don't set the agenda? What will likely happen is that you and your team will lack direction for what must be done on a day-to-day basis, causing confusion, reduced productivity, and disengagement. Since people, like nature, abhor a vacuum (in this case, lack of clear direction), eventually someone will step up and attempt to bring order to the confusion by providing some semblance of direction. That person will quickly become the informal leader and will unofficially usurp your leadership role. People will look to that person for authority and guidance and pay lip service to you. Your boss may then begin to question your value as a leader and wonder whether you are really necessary. At that point your career derailment has begun.

Weak Relationships

- **Failure to nurture relationships and your network.** As I've said previously, relationships make the world go 'round and make all the difference to your day-to-day personal and professional success. In your professional network, there are a number of relationships that are *absolutely critical* to your continued success. These include your relationshp with:

    - your boss

    - your boss's boss

    - your direct reports and team

    - your mentor(s)

    - your sponsor(s)

    - your peers

    - your internal and external customers

    - your HR representative

...to name a few. Similar to relationships in your personal life, building and maintaining strong professional relationships requires conscious thought, careful planning, and ongoing nurturing.

Take a moment to think about the people you spend the most time with at work:

- How would you rate the quality of the relationships you have with them?

- Does the list include people essential to your career success?

- Are these relationships strong enough to help you obtain the resources you need (e.g., time, information, exposure, support, access) to deliver outstanding performance?

Please do not misunderstand me: I firmly believe in mutually beneficial relationships. Every strong relationship involves give and take. What we give and what we get will vary from person to person. But when it comes to career success, we must ensure that a large proportion of our relationships involve give and take that facilitates our delivery of outstanding performance and our effective playing of the game. We may sometimes find ourselves in trouble when we fail to understand the connections between people. Before you sent that angry e-mail, did you pause to consider the relationships that person has with key people in the organization and whether annoying that person could be detrimental to your success?

For example, many people underestimate the power of the administrative staff. Senior executive assistants have direct and regular access to the top leaders in the company who trust their judgment and depend on their network of relationships to gain and disseminate information, cooperation, and support. Wouldn't it be far better for the admins to have a positive perception of you and, better yet, view you as a welcome and contributing member of their network? You will be amazed at the doors that will open when you are part of their network, and the doors that never open when you are not!

- Many people who suffer career derailment close themselves off from others and shut down their network as they work harder and harder to get back on track. If that's your tendency, fight it. In fact, what is much more effective is to make *more* use of your network to help manage or minimize derailment and gain information and support in your turnaround. Your network can:

- Help you understand what made your previous efforts fail.

- Help you gather information on the best way to proceed.

- Coach you on the best way to present your ideas to senior management.

- Provide feedback on your turnaround efforts.

- Help market your successes or provide access to people who can.

- **Positioning yourself to win at the expense of others.** No one likes to feel taken advantage of, and most people dislike others who take all the credit for a team effort. When you find yourself using the word "I" more than the word "we", you are in danger of derailment due to winning at the expense of others. In organizations where team play is a key cultural norm, this will get you into real trouble. You may be perceived as non-collaborative, overtly political, overly-ambitious, and a poor team player.

- **Misusing or abusing power.** With continued success and career advancement comes power. Power is simply the ability to acquire, allocate, or deny resources; in this case, information, jobs, opportunities, exposure, coveted assignments, perks, visibility, access, and so on. Using your power for your own gain and to the detriment of others will typically lead to derailment. An extreme example of this is sexual harassment, which benefits the abuser at the expense of the victim. Another example is to withhold information or resources so that your team wins and another team doesn't, at the expense of the business.

Power and the powerful are seductive. As you gain more and more power, step back and think about how you're using it. Are you on the road to abuse of power and derailment, or are you handling it well?

Signs of Derailment

How can you tell if your career is derailing? In most organizations, there are both formal and informal signs. Typically, the informal signs will be present long before the formal signs. Let's take a look at a few of each.

Informal Signs

- **Increasing isolation: you're not getting information, feedback loops dry up, people avoid you or shut you out.** We all need information in order to do our jobs well. Information is real intelligence that helps us understand what our boss and senior management really want from us, and what are acceptable and unacceptable ways of accomplishing it. If you find yourself feeling invisible, outside of the information loop, and no one is calling or coming to see you, it may be a sign that your input is no longer valued and that you have somehow gone off track. If you find it difficult to obtain feedback about how you are doing, it may be a sign that you are not doing well and no one wants to tell you.

- **Left out of critical meetings a couple of times in a row.** People considered important for the accomplishment of a given task or objective attend critical meetings. If you've been excluded from a couple of critical meetings in a row, you need to examine the importance of your role to the high-priority tasks in your department. The more high priority the task, the closer it is to the organization's "center of gravity." Successful people stay close to the center of gravity.

- **Not invited to participate on important task forces, projects, or assignments.** Task forces are generally set up to address hot topics or opportunities requiring a rapid response. Typically, the company's best experts are assigned to the task force. That puts these task forces at the "center of gravity." If, in recent history, you haven't been assigned to a critical task force that has a role for someone with your expertise, it may be a sign that your value has diminished. Look at the members of the most recent task force. Who was chosen and why? Is there someone on the task force who has your expertise? Why was he or she chosen and not you? Is there a message being sent by your lack of involvement?

- **Your knowledge and expertise are challenged more.** Much of the value and reputation of middle-level and senior executives is determined by their expertise and experience. You are invited to meetings and onto teams and committees because of your knowledge and expertise. When you find your knowledge and expertise repeatedly challenged, particularly by people who never dared do so before, it may be a sign of derailment.

- **Can't get airtime with senior leaders.** In order to be promoted, you and your work must be exposed/visible to senior leaders. If you find that you are rarely or never invited to participate in meetings where senior leaders are present, your visibility and exposure are severely diminished, as is your ability to attract a senior-level sponsor. Without visibility and a sponsor, your career will go nowhere.

- **Tepid response to your presentations from senior management.** Presentations are great opportunities for senior leaders to check out the up-and-coming talent. Since most senior leaders are always on the hunt for good talent, they typically take these opportunities pretty seriously. If when making your presentation you encounter a lot of probing questions, or no questions at all, you might consider you have received a tepid response. If you don't see a lot of heads nodding and smiles in your direction, you're probably receiving a lukewarm response. After the meeting, did anyone pull you aside to ask further questions? Look at the reaction to material presented by someone you know is in your boss's kitchen cabinet. Did you receive a similar reaction? What feedback did you receive from your boss once the meeting concluded?

Formal Signs

- **Low performance rating.** Most companies have some system for rating or grading how well you've accomplished your performance goals. Your performance rating should never be a surprise; you should always be aware of how your boss views your performance and your accomplishments (see Chapter 00). Getting to the top will require consistently receiving either the highest or next highest rating year after year.

  Your performance rating is often linked to your potential rating (how high can you go?), your readiness for promotion, and your salary increase and bonus. A low performance rating is a visible sign of derailment.

- **Lack of promotion or stagnant career growth.** As you look at the career trajectory of your peers, do you seem to be somewhat comparable in your career pace, or have you been in your position longer than anyone else in your department? While promotions slowed during the Great Recession, valued employees are still being promoted or shifted every 3 to 5 years. Every company is different, but every company also has a pattern. What's the pattern in yours? The core members of the boss's kitchen cabinet tend to move the fastest (2 to 3 years), followed by the remaining members of the kitchen cabinet (4 years). Next are the less favored but still highly regarded employees (5 years). The poorly regarded are rarely promoted (6 years or more) and often have to accept a lateral position elsewhere before becoming eligible for promotion.

- **Small, infrequent salary increases.** Astute bosses know that outstanding performers like to be recognized and rewarded for their work or they will move or be lured elsewhere. Thus, the best salary increases and perks go to them. If your salary increase has been average or below average for more than one year (without some other mitigating compensation), it may very well be a sign of derailment. The same applies to below-average incentive compensation and few or no stock or restricted stock options at more senior levels.

Getting Back on Track

It is critical to stop derailment in its tracks. The moment you feel the first inkling that something is not right, stop and assess your situation. This is no time to go into denial. Here are some other things you can do to get back on track:

- **Get candid feedback.** Leverage your network to find out what people (particularly your boss) are thinking and saying about you, your work, and your performance. Find a few trusted allies who will commit to telling you the truth. And then actively listen so you really hear the underlying message. This is the most important step in derailment recovery. You want to listen so you hear and fix the real problem.

- Ask for help and listen to the advice. Once you have accurately identified the problem, you need to determine how best to fix it. Ask for help from people who have solved a similar problem previously, or who are in a good position to help you figure out just how to go about it. Now's the time to consult your mentor(s) and other advocates. Listen to their advice and write it down. Some things they say may not immediately resonate with you but may make more sense later, once you've had more time to think things through, feel a bit calmer, and start moving toward solutions. Explore the pros and cons of different alternatives and look for solutions that have been successful in the past and are consistent with your company's culture and goals.

- **Develop a game plan.** Decide on a solution and develop a detailed action plan to execute. Build in a few quick wins, major milestones, and measures of success so you know when you achieved your turnaround goals and objectives.

You will need regular feedback mechanisms (and thus the ongoing support of your network and mentors) so you can make mid-course corrections if necessary.

- **Your game plan should be completed within a two-to-three-month window.** During this time it will be helpful to strengthen your relationship with your manager, who is the most critical person you have to convince of your improved performance. You will want to achieve demonstrable, measurable, observable change and results as quickly as possible. And it will be important to discreetly market your wins—small, medium and large—as widely as possible. Be sure you strengthen relationships and acknowledge others' contributions by giving credit to everyone involved. Remember, you will not get a second chance to stop the derailment. This is the time to maximize your opportunities and performance.

What if, after all your efforts, your plan doesn't work? At that point you may need to consider a move to another department, division, or branch, or a move to another company, or even to a different city. You might consider a switch in roles. Don't panic and don't give up. It is still entirely possible to recover from derailment in a different environment. Note that it may mean taking a step back in terms of job responsibilities, title, or income, but a step back as part of a clear strategy for moving forward is far better than no step at all.

CHAPTER 12:
How You Leave the Company
Is Important

There will be times in your career when moving forward requires that you move to another company. Since relationships make the world go 'round, how you leave the company is important to your future success. Leaving a company is a little like getting divorced: it can be amicable or acrimonious. Your goal is an amicable parting so that you can leave with your network relatively intact—because you'll undoubtedly need that network later. When your leaving is voluntary, always give the company an opportunity to save face. That typically means allowing them to make a counteroffer, which you will genuinely consider. Both of you may know that, psychologically, you've probably already moved on, but in the spirit of competition (remember this is a game), they want at least one shot at trying to win—that is, retain you. After due consideration, you will gracefully, but regretfully, refuse their counteroffer while maintaining their friendship. If your leave-taking is involuntary, and you go quietly, your company will typically take care of you more generously than if you make a fuss. But if you leave with threats of suing or talking to the media, the company will act to neutralize you (i.e., damage your reputation). By exiting gracefully and without rancor, you can maintain the network of relationships you have worked hard to build over time, which can be of tremendous value and support as you look for a new job or as you seek to produce results in your new job.

The most successful people I know really enjoy their careers and love telling stories about their adventures and misadventures on the way to the top. They used every experience as a learning opportunity and managed to also have a lot of fun. I hope that happens for you as well; that you enjoy your journey to the top and your experiences once you arrive. My very best wishes to you for much continued success.

Index

Made in the USA
San Bernardino, CA
16 November 2017